# THIS IS THE ST

NAMES:_____

AND _____

6 X 6 IN

# TABLE OF CONTENTS

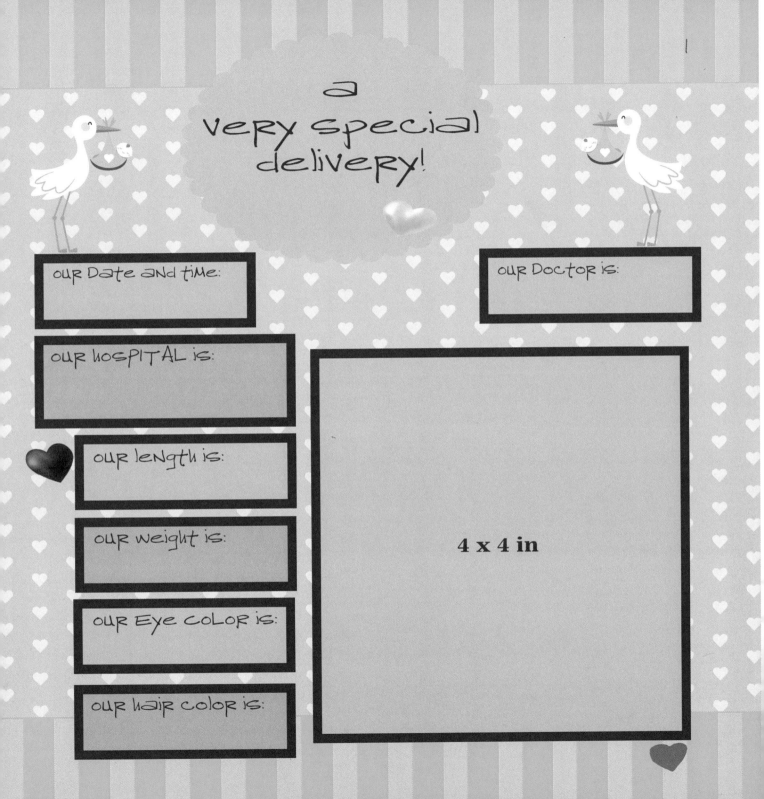

a
very special
delivery!

our Date and time:

our Doctor is:

our hospital is:

our length is:

our weight is:

4 x 4 in

our Eye color is:

our hair color is:

# A letter for the both of you....

# OUR STORY BEGINS

love

SONOGRAM

**4 x 6 in**

# ABOUT MOMMY

FULL BIRTH NAME: _____

DATE OF BIRTH: _____

BIRTH LOCATION: _____

PARENTS: _____

_____

FAVORITE COLOR: _____

FAVORITE FOOD: _____

INTERESTS/HOBBIES/MUSIC/SHOWS: _____

_____

_____

_____

_____

MOM

**4 x 6 in**

## ABOUT DADDY

DAD
4 x 6 in

FULL BIRTH NAME: _____

DATE OF BIRTH:_____

BIRTH LOCATION:_____

PARENTS:_____

_____

FAVORITE COLOR:_____

FAVORITE FOOD:_____

INTERESTS/HOBBIES/MUSIC/SHOWS:_____

_____

_____

_____

_____

# FOOT PRINTS

NAME: _____

RIGHT FOOT

LEFT FOOT

# FOOT PRINTS

NAME: _____

LEFT FOOT

RIGHT FOOT

# HAND PRINTS

NAME: _____

LEFT HAND

RIGHT HAND

# HAND PRINTS

NAME:_____

LEFT HAND

RIGHT HAND

## 1
## MONTH OLD

**Memories & Firsts**

**4 x 6 in**

**1 MONTH OLD**

4 x 6 in

**Memories & Firsts**

# 1
# MONTH OLD

**Memories & Firsts**

4 x 6 in

# 1 MONTH OLD

4 x 6 in

**Memories & Firsts**

# 2
# MONTHS OLD

**Memories & Firsts**

4 x 6 in

**2 MONTHS old**

4 x 6 in

**Memories & Firsts**

# 2
# MONTHS old

**Memories & Firsts**

4 x 6 in

**2**
**MONTHS old**

**Memories & Firsts**

4 x 6 in

18

# 3
# MONTHS old

**Memories & Firsts**

4 x 6 in

# 3
# MONTHS OLD

4 x 6 in

**Memories & Firsts**

# 3
## MONTHS old

**Memories & Firsts**

4 x 6 in

**3**
**MONTHS OLD**

4 x 6 in

**Memories & Firsts**

zz

# 4
# MONTHS old

**Memories & Firsts**

4 x 6 in

# 4 MONTHS OLD

4 x 6 in

## Memories & Firsts

# 4 Months old

**Memories & Firsts**

4 x 6 in

**4
MONTHS old**

4 x 6 in

**Memories & Firsts**

# 5
# MONTHS OLD

**Memories & Firsts**

4 x 6 in

**5
MONTHS old**

**4 x 6 in**

**Memories & Firsts**

# 5
# MONTHS OLD

**Memories & Firsts**

4 x 6 in

**5 MONTHS old**

**Memories & Firsts**

4 x 6 in

# 6
## MONTHS old

### Memories & Firsts

4 x 6 in

**6**

## MONTHS old

4 x 6 in

**Memories & Firsts**

# 6
# MONTHS OLD

**Memories & Firsts**

4 x 6 in

# 6
# MONTHS OLD

4 x 6 in

## Memories & Firsts

# 7
# MONTHS OLD

## Memories & Firsts

4 x 6 in

**7**
**MONTHS OLD**

4 x 6 in

**Memories & Firsts**

# 7
# MONTHS OLD

**Memories & Firsts**

4 x 6 in

**7
MONTHS old**

**4 x 6 in**

**Memories & Firsts**

# 8
# MONTHS old

**Memories & Firsts**

4 x 6 in

**8 MONThS old**

**Memories & Firsts**

4 x 6 in

# 8
# MONTHS OLD

**Memories & Firsts**

4 x 6 in

**8
MONTHS OLD**

**Memories & Firsts**

4 x 6 in

# 9
# MONTHS OLD

**Memories & Firsts**

4 x 6 in

# 9
# MONTHS OLD

**Memories & Firsts**

4 x 6 in

# 9
# MONTHS OLD

**Memories & Firsts**

4 x 6 in

# 9
# MONThS old

**Memories & Firsts**

4 x 6 in

# 10
# MONTHS old

**Memories & Firsts**

4 x 6 in

**10 MONTHS OLD**

4 x 6 in

Memories & Firsts

# 10
# MONThS old

## Memories & Firsts

**4 x 6 in**

**10 MONTHS OLD**

4 x 6 in

**Memories & Firsts**

# 11
# MONTHS OLD

**Memories & Firsts**

4 x 6 in

# 11 MONTHS OLD

**4 x 6 in**

## Memories & Firsts

# 11
## MONTHS OLD

**Memories & Firsts**

4 x 6 in

# 11 MONTHS old

**Memories & Firsts**

4 x 6 in

# 12
# MONTHS OLD

**Memories & Firsts**

4 x 6 in

12

MONThS old

Memories & Firsts

4 x 6 in

# 12
# MONTHS old

## Memories & Firsts

4 x 6 in

# 12 MONTHS OLD

**4 x 6 in**

## Memories & Firsts

# FEEDING TIME

## FAVORITE FOODS:

4 x 6 in

# FEEDING TIME

## FAVORITE FOODS:

4 x 6 in

# BATH TIME

FAVORITE BATH TOYS:

**4 x 6 in**

BATH TIME

4 x 6 in

FAVORITE BATH TOYS:

# PLAY TIME

FAVORITE TOYS:

B
C

4 x 6 in

PLAY TIME

FAVORITE TOYS:

4 x 6 in

# FAMILY TREE

MOM:

DAD:

GRANDMA:

UNCLES:

BROTHER:

SISTER:

GRANDPA:

COUSINS:

AUNTS:

love

# MY FAMILY

FAMILY
PHOTO

**6 x 6 in**

# MY FAMILY

FAMILY
PHOTO

**6 x 6 in**

# MY FAMILY

FAMILY
PHOTO

**6 x 6 in**

NOTES:

NOTES:

# How to add photos to your journal

To add photos to your journal, you'll want to use dry scrapbook adhesives such as glue dots, glue sticks or double -sided tape.  Glue dots are double-sided adhesives that will bond with most any surface.  They're easy to use, aren't messy like other glues and don't require any drying time.  If using glue sticks make sure you Buy quality glue sticks. A glue stick is a great option for adhering lightweight material such as photos.   Inferior glue sticks will quickly dry up and they tend to leave little lumps of glue on your material.  These glue sticks also hold very little glue and will run out twice as fast as quality glue sticks.  Purchase a quality glue stick, such as Elmer's glue stick.   Glue as close to the outside edges of your photos as possible.  You can also use double-sided tape:  permanent  or removable tape.  Double-sided tape is a great way to bond your photo frames to your journal.  Make sure that  the tape is designed for scrapbooking use and is acid-free. In addition to double-sided tape, mounting squares are a good   Mounting squares can be purchased as a roll-on tape dispenser or as sheets which allows you to peel off one square at a time.  Mounting squares work really well for adhering photos to your journal.

# HOW TO PRINT THE HANDS AND FEET

Supplies:
• A bottle of water-based non-toxic fabric paint — many poster paints and finger paints fall into this criteria. Crayola and Kiddie make nice paint sets that you can use for this purpose.
• A few paper plates
• A package of baby wipes
• This Journal

What to do:

Set baby down for a nap in an infant carrier, or transfer to carrier once they fall asleep. Place the carrier on the floor or table. Place fabric paint about the size of a large walnut on a paper plate and smear baby's hand/foot with the paint. Make sure to get paint on each finger/toes, but don't overload the little hand/foot or else the print will be a smeary mess. Don't worry if paint gets under nails — it's non-toxic and will wash off. Before pressing baby's hand onto the journal, try a test print on a piece of paper or another paper plate. You'll want to make sure you've got the right amount of paint to achieve your desired effect. Press the item onto a flattened hand/foot and hold for just a few seconds. It doesn't take long for the aint to transfer. If you're making more than one baby hand/foot print, you may need to reapply the paint. Wipe baby's hands/feet with the baby wipes..